Settlement Of Lands In Edmonton, Enfield, And Elsewhere

SETTLEMENT OF LANDS

IN

Edmonton, Enfield, and elsewhere,

MADE THE 31st OF MAY, 1589,

WITH A VIEW TO THE

MARRIAGE OF ROBERT CECIL, SECOND SON OF WILLIAM, LORD BURGHLEY,

WITH

ELIZABETH BROOKE, DAUGHTER OF WILLIAM, LORD COBHAM.

WITH

SKETCHES OF THE LIVES, AND A PEDIGREE SHEWING THE RELATIONS,
OF THE PARTIES TO THE DEED.

ANNOTATED AND EDITED BY
CHARLES E. B. BOWLES, M.A.

LONDON:
MITCHELL AND HUGHES, 140 WARDOUR STREET, W.

1889.

𝕸arriage 𝕾ettlement

OF

ROBERT, EARL OF SALISBURY, AND ELIZABETH BROOKE, DAUGHTER OF LORD COBHAM.

1589. This Indenture made the laste daye of Maye, in the one and thirtith yere of the raigne of our Soveraigne Ladie Elizabeth by the grace of God, Quene of England France and Ireland, Defender of the Faith etc. Between the Rt. Honble SIR WILLIAM CECILL of the most noble order of the Garter Knight Baron of Burghley, Lord High Treasorer of England and Master of the Courte of Wardes and lyveries on the one partie, and the Right Honorable SIR WILLIAM BROOKE of the said Order of the Garter Knight, Lord Cobham and Lord Wardeyne of the Cynque Portes, HENRY BROOKE Esquier sonne and heire apparannte of the said Lord Cobham, SIR THOMAS CECILL Knight sonne and heire apparan't of the said Lord Burghley EDWARD WOTTON of Boughton Malherbe in the Countie of Kente Esquier WILLIAM FITZWILLIAMS Esquier sonne and heire apparannt of Sir William Fitzwilliams Knight ANTHONY COOKE of Guydehall in the Countie of Essex Esquier FRANCIS BACON of Graies Inne in the Countie of Middlesex Esquier VYNCENT SKYNNER of London gentleman and BARNERD DEWHURST syrvant to the said Lord Burghley on the other partie Witnesseth that whereas It is entended and meante that a mariage shall by the sufferannce of God, be had and solempnized Betwene Robert Cecill Esquier second sonne of the said Baron of Burghley on thone partie and Elizabeth Brooke one of the daughters of the said Lord Cobham on the other partie. Nowe in considerac'on of the said mariage so to be had and solempnized as aforsaid, and for a convenient joincture to be had and assured to the said Elizabeth (yf it shall happen her to overlyve the said Robert Cecill) And for the better advanncement of the said Robert Cecill, and of the heires of the bodie of the said Robert Cecill lawfullie to be begotten and for as muche as the said Robert Cecill is onelie of the half bloud unto Sir Thomas Cecill Knight sonne and heire apparannte of the said Baron of Burghley and for that cause cannot be inheritable as heire to the said Sir Thomas Cecill, nor the said Sir Thomas Cecill to the said Robert Cecill by the lawes of this Realme of any manors lands Tenements or Hereditaments. And for that the said Lord Burghley is mynded to dispose convey and assure all his messuages lands tenements and hereditaments hereafter in theis presents mencioned, and to declare lymyt, and appointe certen uses and entents of the same for the entailling and establyshment of the Inheritannce thereof to remayne to the said Rob' Cecill and his Issue with certen remaynders over hereafter in theis presents expressed And for dyvers and sonndry other good causes and reasonable consideracons the said parties to theis presents especially moving. It is covenanted grannted concluded condiscended and fullie agreed by and betwene the said parties to theis presents in maner and forme following. And the said Baron of Burghley for him his heires and assignes doth covenante promise and grannte to and with the said Lord Cobham Henry Brooke Sir Thos. Cecill Edward Wotton Wm Fitzwilliams Anthony Cooke Franncis Bacon Vyncent Skynner and Barnard Dewhurst their heires and assignes by theis presents that he the said Baron of Burghley before the last day of November next ensueng the date hereof shall and will make and convey or cause to be made and conveyed a good perfecte and sufficient estate or estates in the lawe unto the said Lord Cobham H' Brooke Sir Thos. Cecill Ed. Wotton Wm Fitzwilliams Anthony Cooke Frauncis Bacon Vyncent Skynner and Barnard Dewhurst, and to their heires or to the heires of one of them to the severall uses entents condicons provisoes and lymytacons thereof hereafter in theis presents severallie declared lymited and appointed of and in all and every those his messuage lands tenements and hereditaments hereafter in theis presents mencioned expressed and specified (That is to saie) Of and in all those two farmes and tenements with the appurtenances in Edelmeton alias Edmonnton in the Countie of Middlesex comonly called by the severall name or names of Bury Farme* Calstons Farme alias Caustons Farme and

* Bury Farm, now in the possession of Henry Albany Bowles of Hall Dene, Merrow, near Guildford, youngest son of Humphry Bowles, who had inherited it from his mother, daughter and coheir of Pierce Galliard of Bury Hall, Esq., to whom it had descended from his ancestor

of and in all that Capitall Messuage or Tenement called or knowen by the
name of Pymmes* situate lieng and being in Edelmeton alias Edmonnton
aforsaid And of and in all edifices buildinges barnes stables orchards gardens
lands tenements heriditaments with all and sing'ler their appurtenances to
the saide Farme capital Messuage or tenement or to any of them belonging
or in eny wise apperteyning or occupied letten or used to or with them or
any of them And also of and in one Close of Pasture in the parrishe of
Edmonnton aforesaid conteyning by estemacion six acres comonlie called
Pymmes feilde nere adioyning to the said messuage or tenement called Pymmes
and of and in all that messuage tenement or farme howse comonly called or
knowen by the name of Fuller's Farme situate lieng and beinge in the parrishe
of Edmonnton aforsaid with all and singler the appurtenances and in all edifices
buildings barnes stables orchards gardens lands tenements heriditaments with
all and singler their appurtenances to the said farme messuage or tenement
belonging or in eny wise apperteyning or occupied letten or used to or with
the same or any of them And of and in all that Crofte in the parrishe

Joshua Galliard, who in 1637 bought it, together with Bury Hall at Edmonton, from Euseby
Andrews, whose wife was daughter and sole heir of Jasper Hallam (date of conveyance deed
from Andrews to Galliard 21 April 1637), and this settlement deed on Robert Cecil's marriage I
have no doubt came into my family as a title-deed when this farm was bought. William,
Earl of Salisbury, son of Robert, probably sold it soon after his father's death to Jasper Hallam.
For Pedigree of Galliard and Wills see ' Visitation of London,' Harleian Society, and
' Mis. Gen. et Her.,' Second Series, vol. i., p. 159.
* Pymmes. Of this farm Lysons (' Middlesex,' p. 259), in his article on Edmonton, says :
" Pymmes, which Norden calls a proper little house of the Right Hon[ble] Lord Burleigh, Lord
High Treasurer of England, took its name from the family of Pymme (settled there temp.
Edward II.). It is mentioned among the property of which Robert, Earl of Salisbury, died seised
in 1612." This house was situated on the north side of Watery Lane, and is now entirely
demolished (Robinson's ' History of Edmonton,' p. 60). It is not unlikely that Lord Burghley
lent the house to his daughter and her husband Lord Oxford, as the Registers of Edmonton
testify to the fact that they buried a child there: " Francis Vere fil. Comitis Oxfordiæ sepult
Sep. 12, 1587." (Cansick's ' Epitaphs,' p. xix.)
By an indenture made 16 July 1659 and other deeds in my possession I find that Pymmes,
together with Causton's farm and Waterlees, besides other lands at Edmonton, were settled by
William, Earl of Salisbury, upon his third son Philip Cecil and his children, and appear to have
descended to Arthur Cecil and Maude his wife, of St. Martin's in the Fields, described as a son
of Philip and grandson of Philip above mentioned, and by a deed dated 29 Aug. 1704 to be then
in his possession. In 1659 Pymmes appears to have been leased to Sir John Dackombe and
Dame Melior his wife.

of Edmonnton aforsaid comonlie called or knowen by the name of Drabbes Crofte* conteyning by estimacion foure acres more or lesse And of and in all that Messuage Tenement or Howse with the appurtenance and a garden therunto adjoyninge situate lieng and beinge in Edmonnton aforsaid nere unto the highway there called Caterslowe now or late in the tenure or occupacon of one Robert Cowper or of his assignes And of and in all that feilde or close of land comonlie called Waterlees† conteyning by estimacon foure acres more or lesse lieng in Edmonnton aforsaid sometyme in the occupacon of Emme Ogle widowe and now or late in the tenure or occupacon of Jasper Leake Esquier or of his assignes And of and in all that farme and all those messuages lands tenements and hereditaments with the appurtenances situate lieng and being in Edmonnton aforsaid which late were the Inheritannce of one William Morgan of the parrishe of Sanct Mary Matfellon alias Whitechappell without Algate gent and now or late in the severall tenures or occupacons of one Thomas Gervis and Richard Wylde or of one of them their or one of their assignee or assignes And of and in all those two little groves or closes of pasture in Edmonnton aforsaid with the appurtenance comonlie called or knowne by the name of Cuckowe groves‡ now or late in the tenure or occupacon of . . . . Sare widowe And of and in that one close of pasture with the appurtenances in Edmonnton aforsaid called Peverells now or late in the tenure or occupacon of Robert Larkyn alias Estrey And of and in those severall parcells of land with the appurtenances in Edmonnton aforsaid ymediatlie hereafter followinge (that is to say) seaven acres and an half of land more or lesse in the hide§ in Edmonnton aforsaid half an acre of land more or lesse in

---

* Drabbes Crofte. See note on Land in the Hide.

† Waterlees sold by William, Earl of Salisbury, January 1614, to Everard Fawkener.

‡ Cuckowe Groves. In the schedule of lands given by Robinson in his 'History of Edmonton,' pp. 254, 284, etc., mention is made of Cuckoo Hall Farm House and lands, no doubt the pasture lands called Cuckowe Groves settled on Robert Cecil.

§ Land in the Hide. The Hyde or Hide appears to have been divided in 1819 among several small landowners. A portion belonged to the Galliards of Bury Hall, and descended to Mary, daughter and coheir of Pierce Galliard (the last of that family), who, after the death of her husband Charles Bowles (High Sheriff for Surrey 1794), sold it. The portion settled on Robert Cecil is mentioned, together with the land, in the field called " Storksnest," in a deed of feofment from William, Earl of Salisbury, to Edward Nowell, dated 20 January 1613 (in my possession), and is described as " one acre more or less in the said Comon feilde called the Hide adjoining North along the King's Highway leading from Edmonton Church by the said parsonage house,

Starcksnest* in Edmonnton aforsaid Thre acres of lande more or less in TYLBARONGES Feilde in Edmonnton aforsaid one acre of land more or lesse in HAGFEILDE† in Edmonnton aforsaid and two acres of land more or lesse in the comon marshe of Edmonnton aforsaid late in the tenure or occupacion of one Geffrey Wakkedon gent or his assignes And of and in all those Four-score and two acres and one roode of meadowe more or lesse lieng and being in the comon marshe of Edmonnton aforsaid now or late in the tenure or occupacion of one John Taillor and .... Stoddarde or their or the one of their assignee or assignes And of and in all that messuage or Ten't with the appurtenances called or knowen by the name of PLEASANTYNES‡ scituate lieng and being in Edmonnton aforsaid now or late in the tenure or occupacion of one William Dowgill And of and in all that Mannor or farme of DEPEHAMS§ in the parrishe of Edmonnton aforsaid with the rightes

towards the Church of Enfeilde." This Deed, which is signed by "Wm Salesbury," in the presence of "Henry Hobarte," Bart. (Sir Henry, created a baronet 1611, is ancestor to the Earl of Buckinghamshrie), further states that William, Earl of Salisbury, having sold to Edward Nowell a water mill with its appurtenances, covenants to permit the said Edward Nowell to make "a convenient overshott in the ground of the said Wm Earl of Salisbury in the place where the overshott was of late made in a close called Drabbes Crofte for turning of water for use of the said mill."

Robinson (p. 5) describes it as a large field of about 290 acres near the church at Edmonton, and is said to have been originally obtained of one of the kings by a lady who begged of him such a piece of land as she could encompass with a bull's hide, which the king readily granted, when the lady, ordering a bull's hide to be dried and tanned, contrived to cut it into so many lengths that when joined together encompassed the field; hence its name.

* Starcksnest or Starksnest (see also note § p. 6) appears to have been divided among three or four owners in 1809, and a portion of it was sold in 1800, with other lands (Robinson, p. 234), by the Commissioners, to raise a sufficient sum to defray the expenses of passing an Act for dividing and surveying the common lands and marshes, etc.

† Hagfield also seems to have been possessed by several small owners in 1809.

‡ Pleasantynes. Lysons (p. 259) says: "The Cecils had another farm called Pleasantines, a corruption perhaps of Plessyngton, the name of a family who had considerable property in Edmonton in the time of Edward III., which still goes by that name, and some lands, parcel of the manor formerly the property of William, Lord Paget, and granted to Lord Salisbury by James I. anno 1608. Pleasantines has been held with the manor of Deephams ever since Lord Burghley's death, and is now the property of Mrs. Cock."

§ Manor of Depehams, now called Deephams Farm, took its name from Roger de Depeham, who made various purchases at Edmonton temp. Edward III. It was bought and sold several times until it became the property of Thomas Wroth, who sold it in 1588 to William, Lord Burghley

liberties members and appurtenances thereof And of and in all and
singuler messuages lands Tent's and Hereditaments to the said messuage
mannor or farme belonging or in eny wise apperteyning or occupied or used
to or with them or either of them.   And of and in all and singuler the
wood grounds woods and underwoods with the appurtenances of the said
Lord Burghley lieng and being in Edmonnton aforsaid Tottenham and
Enfeilde in the said Countie of Middlesex or in any of them And of and in
all other the frehoulde lands ten'tes and hereditaments etc. of the said Lord
Burghley in Edmonnton and Tottenham aforsaid or in any of them And of
and in the Scite circuit precincte of the late priory or howse of Nunnes of
Ladie Swetmanscrofte otherwise called Chesthunte alias Chestrehunt
Nunry* in the Countie of Hertff.   And of and in all and singuler lands
tenements fisshinges Rentes revercions syrvices and Hereditaments whatsoever
with all and singler their appurtenances of the said Baron of Burghley in the
Counties of Hertff. and Essex or either of them heretofore parcell of the
possessions of the said Priory or nunrye And of and in one yerelie rent of
Tenne quarters of wheate yssueng out of the mannor of Rothing or High

(the year before the date of settlement), and it was sold in 1628 by his grandson William, Lord
Salisbury, to Thomas Style, from whom it descended by intermarriage to the Ravencrofts, who
sold it in 1789 to Thomas Cock, whose son is the present owner (1809).   The house is moated, and
was formerly the residence of the Bohuns, Earls of Hereford.   (Lysons, p. 257; Robinson, p. 55.)

* Scite circuit and lands belonging to the late Priory of Lady Swetmanscroft alias
Cheshunt Nunnery, co. Herts.   Chauncey (vol. i., p. 586) gives the following: " The Nunnery
near the river Lea, which the Canons of Cathels did anciently possess, but King Henry III.
removed them anno 24 Regii sui, granted it to the Prioress and Nuns of Chesthont to hold of
him and his heirs to them and their successors in free, pure, and perpetual alms, and at
the time of the dissolution hereof it was valued in the Exchequer to be yearly worth £27 6s. 8d.
and came to the Crown.   King Edward VI. granted this manor to Anthony Denny, Esq., to
hold of the King by the yearly rent of 40s., from whom it passed to Henry Denny his son and
heir, and from him to Edward, Lord Denny, Earl of Norwich, who sold it to Robert Dewhurst,
Esq., Custos Rotulorum of the King's Bench, but he dying without issue gave it to Anne Gill,
who conveyed it on her death to Anne Gill her mother, from whom it descended to John Gill her
son and heir, who sold it to John Mortimer, the present possessor."

Stephens, in his additions to Dugdale's 'Monasticon' (vol. i., p. 526, edition 1722), gives
this further information : "That it appears to have been a cell to the Monastery of Canons at
Catteley in Lincolnshire, and dedicated to the Blessed Virgin.   Henry III. removed those
Canons, and gave this House to the Nuns of St. Benedict.   (For Charter see vol. i., p. 512,
edition 1655.)   In 1103 the Pope exempted the site of the House with all its lands, etc., from
payment of tithes.   The Nuns enjoyed this Priory till the suppression.   In 1553 a pension of

Rothing in the said Countie of Essex late parcell of the possessions of the said Priory And of and in all that messuage or farme called the dairie howse with the appurtenances situate in Enfeilde aforsaid and of and in all lands to the same belonging or occupied to or with the same And of and in one close of arrable lande called Reynerds feilde being in Enfield aforsaid and one acre of meadowe by estimacion lieing and being in Wyldemarshe with the appurtenances situate lieing and being in the parishe of Enfeilde in the Countie of Middlesex and in the parrishe of Chesthunte in the Countie of Hertff. or in any or either of them sometymes parcell of the mannor of Worcetor* in

£5 was paid to one Margaret Hill, who perhaps was the last Prioress." From the time that it became Crown property the account differs little from that of Chauncey.

These authorities are evidently wrong in the fact that Lord Denny sold it to Robert Dewhurst, because here we find it possessed by Lord Burghley, forty-five years before the Visitation of Herts, which asserts that it belonged to Robert Dewhurst. Lord Burghley may have bought it from Lord Denny, or it is possible that he bought it together with the manor and park of Cheshunt, which I find, from 'Mis. Gen. et Her.' (New Series, vol. iv., pp. 191, 207, and 208), was bought by Lord Burghley from Henry Denny in 1570, who bought it from John Harrington the 31st October 1567, and Robert Cecil, or his son William, may have sold it to his father's old servant. It is worthy of note that this deed, though settling Cheshunt Priory, does not include the manor of Theobalds, also in the parish of Cheshunt, and which also descended to Robert Cecil on his father's death, and was his usual place of residence, as it was also his father's, for some little time after Lord Burghley's death, until James I., who had been twice entertained by his Secretary there, took a fancy to the place; when Robert Cecil exchanged it with his sovereign for the palace at Hatfield, the residence of his descendant and representative the present Marquis of Salisbury. It then became a favourite residence of the King, who considerably enlarged the park, and occasionally his son Charles resided there, but it was entirely pulled down by the order of the Parliament during the Civil Wars. (Lysons' 'Herts,' p. 30.)

Lysons has not given the year in which Lord Burghley bought Theobalds, but states that, having bought it, he, in the year 1560, built an entirely new house as a residence for Robert Cecil, and there entertained Queen Elizabeth in 1564, comparing which dates with that of 1570 given above as the year in which the manor and park of Cheshunt were bought, it would seem, if Lysons is right, that Theobalds was bought considerably before the rest of the Chesthunt property, concerning which latter conveyance the final indenture is not signed before Trinity term 12 Elizabeth.

* Lands belonging to the manor of Worcestors. This manor belonged to John de Enefelde who died 1350. His widow married John Wroth, to whom Francis son and heir of John de Enefelde sold the manor; and it remained in the Wroth family, under the name of Wroth's Place, till in 1413 it passed to Sir John Tiptoft, cousin to the Wroths. John Tiptoft, Lord Powys (jure uxoris), died 1443, and the manor was inherited by his son John, created 1449 Earl of Worcester, Chancellor of Ireland in the reign of Edward IV. By intermarriage it passed

B

Enfeilde aforsaid. And it is further agreed betwene the said parties to theis presents And it is the full entent and meaning of the said parties to theis presents that the said conveyance and assurance of the premises or any parte thereof hereafter before the said last daie of November next ensueng the date hereof to be had or made by the said Baron of Burghley or any other person or persons to the said Lord Cobham Henry Brooke Sir Thomas Cecill Edward Wotton William Fitzwilliams Anthony Cooke Franncis Bacon Vyncent Skynner and Barnerd Dewhurst and to their heirs or to the heirs of any of them by what name or names soever the premisses or any parte thereof or the parties to the said conveiance and assurannce or any of them shalbe named or called ymediatlie from the having or making thereof shalbe And that the said person and persons to whome the said conveiances and assurances or any of them shalbe so had or made and his and their heires ymediatlie from the tyme of the having or making thereof shall stand and be seised for ever of the Premisses and of everie parte and parcell thereof to the severall use or uses ententes lymitacions provises and condicions thereof hereafter in theis presents lymited declared mencioned or expressed and in suche maner and forme as the severall use and uses therof and of every parte and parcell thereof be hereafter in theis presents lymited appointed set fourth or declared and to none other use entent, or purpose That is to saye of and in all the said farmes and tene[ts] with the appurtenances in Edmonnton aforsaid comonlie called by the severall names of Bury Farme and Calstones Farme alias Cawstons farme and also of and in all other the said messuages farmes messuages tene'ts meadowes feadings pastures and hered'ts with the appurt'ces before in theis pres'ts expressed situate lieng and being in the Mannor Towne parrishe or feilde of Edmonnton aforsaid (except the said messuage called Pleasantynes and the said manor or farme of Depehams with the appurten'ces aforsaid and all lands ten'ts and hered'ts aforsaid to the said messuage manor or farme or either of them belonging and except all the said

<hr />

into the possession of several families, till it fell into the hands of the Earl of Rutland, who in 1540 gave it to Henry VIII., and his son Edward VI. settled it on his sister Elizabeth. (Lysons, p. 292.)

Lysons goes on to say that it was granted by Elizabeth or James to Robert, Lord Salisbury, but at what time he could not say; but that in 1635 it was the property of Sir Nicholas Raynton, from whom it passed by intermarriages through the families of Wolstonholme and Breton till it was sold in 1785 to Edmond Armstrong.

woodgroundes woods and underwoods in Edmonnton Tottenham and Enfeilde To the use and behouff of the said Rob[t] Cecill and of the said Elizabeth Brooke for her Joyncture and of the heires of the bodie of the said Rob[t] Cecill lawfullie to be begotten. And for default of suche Issue Then of and in one full thirde parte of all and singuler the said farmes messuages lands tenements and hered'ts and other the premisses in Edmonnton aforsaid (except before excepted) to the use and behouff of the ladie Elizabeth Veer eldest daughter of the right Honorable Edwarde Earle of Oxforde and of Ladie Anne late his wife deceased and of the heires of the bodie of the said Ladie Elizabeth lawfullie to be begotten And for defaulte of suche Issue to the use of the Ladie Bridget Veer and the Ladie Susan Veer two other of the daughters of the said Earle of Oxforde and of the heires of their two bodies lawfullie to be begotten and for default of suche Issue to the use of the heires of the bodie of the said Lord Burghley lawfullie begotten And for default of such Issue to the use of the right heires of the said Baron of Burghley for ever And of and in one other full third parte of all and singuler the said farmes messuages lands tent's and Hereditaments and other the Premisses in Edmonnton aforsaid (except before excepted) To the use and behouff of the said Ladie Bridget Veer second daughter of the said Edward Earle of Oxforde and of the said Ladie Anne late his wife and of the heires of the bodie of the said Lady (*sic*) Bridget lawfullie to be begotten And for default of suche Issue to the use of the said Ladie Elizabeth Veer and ladie Susan Veer and of the heires of their two bodies lawfullie to be begotten And for default of suche Issue to the use of the heires of the bodie of the said Lord Burghley lawfullie begotten And for defaulte of suche Yssue to the use of the right heires of the said Baron of Burghley for ever And of and in one other full third parte of all and singular the said farms messuages lands Tent's and Hered'ts and other the premisses in Edmonnton aforsaid (except before excepted) To the use and behouff of the Ladie Susan Veer yongest daughter of the said Edward Erle of Oxford and of the said Ladie Anne late his wife and of the heires of the body of the said Ladie Susan lawfullie to be begotten And for default of such yssue to the use of the said Ladie Elizabeth Veer and Ladie Bridget and of the heires of their two bodies lawfullie to be begotten And for default of suche Issue to the use of the heires of the bodie of the said Lord Burghley lawfullie begotten And for defaulte of suche Issue to the use of the righte heires of the said Lord Burghley forever And of and in the said Scite circuit and presincte of the said late Priory or Howse of Nunnes of Swetmanscrofte alias Chesthunt alias Chestrehunt Nunnrie in the Countie of Hertff. aforesaid and of and in all other the messuages lands tenem^{ts} and herdit^{ts} aforsaid with the appurtenances heretofore parcell of the possessions of the said Pryorie or Nunry and of and in the said Tenne quarters of wheat to the use of the said Lord Burghley for and during his naturall lief without ympechement of waste. And after his decease To the use of the said Robert Cecill for terme of his naturall lief. And afterward to the use and behouff of the said Elizabeth Brooke for and during her naturall lyfe for an augmentac'on of her said Joincture (yf the said Robert Cecill shall at the tyme of his decease have any childe lyving by him upon the bodie of the said Elizabeth Brooke begotten or yf she the said Elizabeth Brooke shall at such tyme of his death be enseint with childe by him. And for default of suche Issue and of being enseint Then to the use of the said Robert Cecill and the heires of his bodie lawfullie begotten. And for default of suche Issue of one full thirde parte of the said Scite and other the premises last abouemencioned to the use and behouff of the said Ladie Elizabeth Veer and of the heires of her bodie lawfullie to be begotten And for default of suche Issue to the use of the said Ladie Bridget Veer and Ladie Susan Veer and of the heires of their two bodies lawfullie to be begotten. And for defaulte of suche Issue to the use of the heires of the bodie of the said Lorde Burghley lawfullie begotten And for default of such Issue to the use of the right heires of the said Lord Burghley for ever. And in one other full thirde parte of the said Scite and other the premises last abouemencioned to the use and behouff of the said Ladie Bridget Veer and of the heires of her bodie lawfullie to be begotten. And for default of such Issue to the use of the said Ladie Elizabeth Veer and Ladie Susan Veer and of the heires of their two bodies lawfullie to be begotten. And for default of suche Issue to the use of the heires of the bodie of the said Lorde Burghley lawfullie begotten. And for default of suche Issue to the use of the right heires of the said Lord Burghley forever. And of and in the said messuage called Pleasantynes and the said Mannor of Depehams with the appurtenances aforsaid and of and in all and singler the lands tenements and hereditaments to the said messuage or mannor or either of them belonging. And of and in all and singler the said woodgrounds woods and underwoods of the said Lord Burghley situate lieing and being in Edmonton Tottenham and Enfeilde aforsaid or in any of them with all and singler th'appurtenances And of and in the said messuage or farme called the Dairy house with th'appurtenances and other the premisses sometyme parcell of the mannor of Wourcetors in Enfeilde aforsaid and of and in all other the lands tent' and heredt' of the said Lord Burghley in Edmonnton Tottenham and Enfeilde aforsaid or any of them whereof noe use or uses is or are before in theis presents lymyted or declared To the use and behouff of the said Lord Burghley for and during his naturall lief without ympechement of waste And after his decease then to the use and behouff of the said Robert Cecill and of the heires of his bodie lawfullie to be begotten and for default of such Issue of and in one full third parte of all and singular the said messuage called Pleasantynes and of the said mannor or farme of Depehams aforsaid and of the said woodgrounds woods and underwoods and of all other the said last abouemencioned premisses to the use and behouff of the said Lady Elizabeth Veer and of the heires of her bodie lawfullie to be begotten And for default of such Issue to the use of the said Ladie Bridget Veer and Ladie Susan Veer and of the heires of their two bodies lawfullie begotten And for default of such Issue to the use of the heires of the bodie of the said Lord Burghley lawfullie begotten And for default of suche Issue to the use of the right heires of the said Lord Burghley for ever And of and in one other full thirde parte of the same last mencioned premisses to the use and behouff of the said Ladie Bridget Veer and of the heires of her bodie lawfullie to be begotten And for default of such Issue to the use of the said Ladie Elizabeth Veer and Ladie Susan Veer and of the heires of their two bodies lawfullie to be begotten And for default of such Issue To the use and behouff of the heires of the bodie of the said Lorde Burghley lawfullie begotton And for default of such Issue to the use and behouff of the right heires of the said Lord Burghley for ever. And of and in one other full third parte of the said last mencioned premisses to the use and behouff of the said Ladie Susan Veer and of the heires of her bodie lawfullie to be begotten and for default of such Issue to the use of the said Ladie Elizabeth Veer and Ladie Bridget Veer and of the heires of their two bodies lawfullie to be begotten And for default of such Issue to the use and behouff of the heires of the bodie of the said Lord Burghley lawfullie begotten And for default of such Issue to the use and behouff of the right heires of the said Lord Burghley for ever. Provided alwaies that if in the lief tyme of the said Lord Burghley yt shall happen the said Robert Cecill to decease leaving yssue alyve by him on the bodie of the said Elizabeth Brooke lawfullie begotten or otherwise leaving the said Elizabeth Brooke enseinte with childe by him That then the said use before by theis presents lymited to him the said Lord Burghley of the said Nunnrie or Priory of Chesthunte and of the Premisses belonging to the said Priory shall ymediatlie cease during all the lief of the said Elizabeth Brooke And shalbe and veste ymediatlie in her the said Elizabeth Brooke during her lief Any thing or matter before in theis presents conteyned to the contrarie thereof in eny wise notwithstonding. Provided alwais that if the said Elizabeth Brooke shall happen to survyve the said Robert Cecill and shall disagree and refuse to accept have or take the said lands tenements and hered[ts] before by theis presents lymited appointed or meant to be conveied for her Jointure, and the augmentacion of her Jointure and also shall not take any benefit thereof That then she the said Elizabeth shalbe at libertie to forsake and refuse the said Joincture and augmentacion of Joincture and to take her dower of and in the Manors lands Tent's and Heredit[ts] of the said Robert Cecill whereof he shalbe seised at the tyme of his decease of any estate of Inheritannce This Indenture or any matter or thing herein conteyned To the contrarie thereof in any wise notwithstanding. Provided also and nevertheles It is covenanted grannted condiscended and agreed betwene the said parties to theis pres'nts That all and everie the said uses and lymytacions of uses and estates before in theis presents lymyted appointed raised conveied or entended or meante to the said Robert Cecill and to the heires of his body and to the said Thre daughters of the said Ladie Anne late Countesse of Oxford and to the heires of their bodies shall as towching onelie the said Robert Cecill and his ymediate sonnes and daughters and the said Thre daughters of the said Erle of Oxford and their and everie of their ymediat sonnes and daughters stand and be upon the lymytacons hereafter in theis pres'nts expressed That is to saie yf the said Robert Cecill or any the ymediate sonne or sonnes daughter or daughters of him the said Robert or if the said Ladie Elizabeth Veer or the said Ladie Bridget Veer or the said Ladie Susan Veer or any the ymediate sonne or sonnes daughter or daughters of them or any of them that hath or shall have any estate righte or title in the Premisses or any parte thereof by the trewe entent or meaning of theis presents at anye tyme or tymes hereafter shall determynatlie consent or attempte to doe knoledge or suffer any acte or thing whatsoever which upon the full execucion thereof shall or may be any barre alteracon forfeiture determynacon or discontynuance of any parte of the Intaille herein before lymited or of the frehoulde or Inheritannce of the premisses or any parte thereof or whereby any use or uses by theis presents lymited entended or appointed or any the estate or estates or right that should arrise or come by reason of theis presents and of the conveiance and assurance aforsaid or any of them shalbe altered determyned undon debarred forfeited or discontynued or shall by any meanes charge or Incumber the same premisses or any parte thereof with any Rente or Rentes or other estates charges or Incumbrannces to the preiudice hurte or detryment of any person or persons to whome the premisses or any parte thereof should discende revert remayne or come by the trewe entente and meaning of theis presents or whereby the trewe entent and meaninge of theis presents may not or cannot take place or effecte That then and from thenforth and ymediatlie from and after the tyme of suche consenting or attempting and before any such barre alteracion forfeiture determynacon or discontynuance had made suffered or don All and every the use and uses estate and estates lymited and declared in and by theis presentes as to him or them onelie which shall so attempte or consente to or for any suche acte or actes thing or things to be had donne knoledged or suffered contrarie to the trewe entent and meaning of theis presents of and in suche and so muche of the premisses whereof any suche consente or attempte shalbe, shall cease and determyne onelie as in respecte and having regarde to suche person and persons so attempting or consenting in suche sorte degree qualitie and condicion as if suche person or persons so attempting or consenting were naturally deade and not other-wise And that then and from thenforth from tyme to tyme suche and somuche of the premises whereof any suche consent or attempte shalbe so had made or don shalbe ymediatlie to suche person and persons to whome by the lymytacions of the uses aforsaid the same shoulde have remayned come or bene according to the trewe entente and meaning of theis presents of and in suche estate degree and condicion as in theis presents is expressed lymyted entended or mencioned and with such remaynders thereof over and with suche lymytacions proviso and condicions as are thereof in theis presents expressed or lymyted as if suche person or persons that soe shall consente or attempte to or for any suche acte or thing to be don at and ymediately before suche consentinge or attempting had byn naturallie deade and not otherwise. And that the said conveiannce and assurance soe as is aforesaid appointed to be made to the said Lord Cobham Henry Brooke Sir Thomas Cecill Edward Wotton William Fitzwilliams Anthony Cooke Franncis Bacon Vyncent Skynner and Barnerd Dewhurste and their heires or to the heires of one of them And everie other conveiance and assurance to be had made or suffered by the said Baron of Burghley to the said Lord Cobham Henry Brooke Sir Thomas Cecill Edward Wotton William Fitz-williams Anthony Cooke Frannces Bacon Vyncent Skynner and Barnard Dewhurste or any of them of the said messuages lands tenements and hereditaments or any parte thereof to be had or made before the said last daie of November ymediatlie from thenfforth shalbe. And the said Lord Cobham Henry Brooke Sir Thomas Cecill Edward Wotton William Fitz-williams Anthony Cooke Franncis Bacon Vyncent Skynner and Barnard Dewhurste and their heires shall also ymediatlie from thenfforth and from tyme to tyme after stand and be seised of and in such partes and so muche of the said messuages lands tenements and hereditaments for or confyrming the which any of the said actes matters or thinges aforsaid shall either be so attempted practised procured caused or comannded to be don orells deter-mynatlie assented or willingly suffered to be attempted or gon aboute by any open acte or deed to be executed don performed or put in use as is aforsaid to suche and the same use and uses and to suche and the same person and persons as by force of theis presents after the decease of suche person so attempting to doe any suche acte or deed ought to have and enioy the same and in suche and the same maner forme qualitie and condicion to everie entente confirmacion and purpose as if the same person or persons and everie of them that so shall consent attempte or goe aboute by enny open acte or deed to doe cause or suffer any suche thinge to be don were then deade and as though the said devises actes matters and thinges had never byn don attempted procured caused had made or suffered to be don Any thinge in theis presents conteyned or any other matter or cause what-soever to the contrarie thereof in eny wise notwithstonding Provided never-theles and it is coven'nted condiscended and agreed by and betwene the said parties to theis presents That if it shall fortune suche one of the said persons that hath or shall have any estate right or title in the premisses or any parte thereof by the trewe entent and meaning of theis presents as shall have no yssue in being borne and alyve of his or her bodie lawfullie begotten at any tyme hereafter determynatelie to assente suffer procure comitt or doe any thinge or acte or assent to or for any thing or acte to be don whereby any use by theis presents to be to him or her lymited shall ende discontynue be voied or of none effecte by the provisoe last aforsaid That yet nevertheles assoone as suche one of the said parsons that hath or shall have any estate right or title in the premisses or any parte thereof by the trewe entent and meaning of theis presents as having no yssue in being borne and alyve of his or her bodie lawfullie begotten shall fortune at any tyme hereafter so to assent suffer or procure comitt or doe any thing or acte or assente to or for anything or acte to be don whereby any estate or use by theis presents to him or her lymited shall end determyne be void and of none effecte by the provisoe last aforsaid shall then afterward happen to have yssue of his or her bodie lawfullie begotten That then and ymediatlie after the birth of suche Issue the use and uses vested upon any the acts in the aforsaid provisoe last above said shall ccase And that then and from thenfforth the use and uses of and in suche and somuche of the said messuages ffarmes landes tene'nts and premisses for or consyrning the whiche any of the things aforsaid mencioned in the said proviso shalbe so attempted caused procured comannded assented or suffered to be executed performed don or put in use or gon aboute to be executed performed don or put in use by the father or mother of suche childe contrarie to the trewe meaninge of theis presents shalbe to suche childe and the heires of the bodie of the same childe lawfullie begotten And for default of such Issue to the use and behouff of everie suche person and persons as at any tyme hereafter shalbe heire of the bodie of suche one of the persons that hath or shall have any estate right or title in the premisses or any parte thereof by the trewe entent and meaning of theis presents as having no childe in being borne and alyve of his or her bodie lawfullie begotten shall fortune at any tyme hereafter so to assent suffer or procure comitt or doe any acte or thinge or so assente to or for any acte or thinge to be don whereby the use by theis presents to him or her lymited shall end determyne cease, be voied, or of none effecte by the proviso afore-said touching the same with the Remaynders thereof over in use in maner and forme before expressed and lymyted Provided nevertheles that it shall and may be lawfull to and for the said Robert Cecill Ladie Elizabeth Veer Lady Bridget Veer and Lady Susan Veer and to and for the Heires of their and everie of their bodies being in possession of the premisses by vertue

of theis presents and of the said assurannce and conveiance and being of the
aige of one and twentie yeres or aboue by his her or their deede or deeds
Indented to demise grannte and to ferme lett at his her and their fre will
and pleasure all and everie the landes tenements and hereditaments aforsaid
except the said Scite Circuit and presincte of the said late priorie or house of
Nunnes of Ladie Swetmanscrofte otherwise called Chesthunte alias
Chestrehunte Nunrie in the Countie of Hertff. aforsaid and except all and
singler lands tenements ffisshings rents revercions syrvice and hereditaments
whatsoever with all and singler their appurtenances of the said Baron of
Burghley in the said Counties of Hertff. and Essex or either of them
heretofore parcell of the possessions of the said Priorie or Nunrie and except
the said yerelie rent of Tenne quarters of wheate aforesaid To any person or
persons in possession onelie and not in revercion for the terme of one and
twentie yeres or for and during any terme not exceading the nomber of one
and twenty yeres at his her and their will and pleasyr So that the rents and
syrvice presentlie resyrved and yerelie to be due and paiable for the same or
more or the accustomed rent or rentes for suche and somuche of the Premisses
or suche parte or parcell thereof as shalbe so demised or grannted shalbe
resyrved and paiable for and during the contynuance of the said lease and
leases grannt or granntes so thereof to be made or grannted And that the use
of everie suche parte and parcell of the premisses as shalbe so demised or
grannted shalbe to everie suche person and persons to whome any suche
demise or grannte shalbe made as aforsaid their executors administrators and
assignes onelie for and during the contynuance of the estate and estates
terme and termes Interest and Interests to be lymited and expressed in such
demise and grannts according to the purporte and trewe meaning of everie
suche demise and grannte Any thinge or matter whatsoever to the contrarie
thereof in eny wise notwithstonding Provided alwaies that if any suche
person or persons to whome any suche demise or grannte shalbe made as is
aforsaid his or their executors administrators or assignes or any of them
shall not yerelie during the contynuance of the said terme and termes well
and truly paie or cause to be paied to him or them to whome the ymediate
revercion or remaynder of suche parte and parcell of the premisses so to be
demised as aforsaid for the tyme being shall belong and be by the
lymitacion entent and trewe meaning of theis presents The Rents and syrvices
resyrved by the said Indentures at suche tymes and places as by the said

Indentures shalbe lymited or shall doe suffer or comit upon suche parte or parcell of the premisses as shalbe letten or grannted to him or them any waste to the value of forty shillinges That then all and everie estate and estates made granted or created to any suche person or persons not paieng or doing their rentes and syrvices resyrved in maner and forme aforesaid or making any such wast as aforsaid shalbe utterlie voied and determyned. And that from thenceforth the said Lord Cobham Henry Brooke Sir Thos. Cecill Edward Wotton Wm Fitzwilliams Anth^y Cooke Frannces Bacon Vyncent Skynner and Barnard Dewhurst and their heires shall stand and be seised of all and everie suche Lands Tenements and Hereditaments whereof the rentes shall not be paied as aforesaid or whereof any wast shalbe don in maner and forme aforsaid to suche ententes and purposes as if noe suche demise or lease had byn made of any suche lands tenements and hereditaments whereof the said Rente shall not be paied as is aforesaid or any wast donne in maner and forme aforsaid. And further the said Baron of Burghley for the consideracion aforsaid for him his heires and assignes doth covennante promise and grannte to and with the said Lord Cobham Henry Brooke Sir Thos. Cecill Edward Wotton Wm Fitzw^ms Anthony Cooke Frannces Bacon Vyncent Skynner and Barnard Dewhurst their heires and assignes by theis presents That if the said Baron of Burghley before the said laste daie of November next ensuenge the date hereof doe not make a good perfecte and lawfull estate conveiance and assurannce of all and everie the said mannors messuages lands tenements and hereditaments and of everie parte thereof unto the said Lord Cobbam Henry Brooke Sir Thos. Cecill Ed. Wotton William Fitzwilliams Anthony Cooke Frannces Bacon Vyncent Skynner and Barnard Dewhurste their heires and assignes or to the heires of one of them to the severall uses and intents before in theis presents expressed That then and at all tymès from and after the said last daie of November he the said Baron of Burghley and his heires and assignes and all and everie other person and persons that now be or hereafter shalbe seised of the said mannors messuages lands Tenements and heredit^ts before in theis presents mencioned or of any parte or parcell thereof of any estate of Inheritannce shall stand and be thereof and of every parcell thereof seised and all estates conveiances and assurances by fyne feoffemente recoverie or otherwise heretofore made or hereafter to be made of the said Messuages Lands Tenements and Hereditaments or of any parte thereof shalbe to suche the severall uses entents lymitacions condicions and agreaments and to and of suche severall persons and for and of such severall estates and uses and under suche provisoes condicons and lymitacons as are in theis presentes lymited expressed named and declared and to none other uses ententes or purposes Any matter or cause to the contrary notwithstonding Provided alwaies and nevertheles It is condiscended and agreed betwene the said parties to theis presents That if the said Baron of Burghley at any tyme or tymes hereafter during his lief by his writing or writings by him subscribed and sealed with his seale do signefie or declare that his mynd will and pleasure is That the severall uses and ententes and lymitacons of uses and estates in theis presents declared lymited or expressed or any of them except the uses and ententes and lymitacons of uses and estates in theis presents declared lymited or expressed to the said Robert Cecill and Elizabeth Brooke and to the heires of the bodie of the said Robert Cecill or to any of them shalbe voied and of none effecte either towching or concerning all the aforsaid mannors lands tenements and hereditaments and other the premises before in theis presents mencioned or towching or concerning any parte or parcell of them or any of them That then and from thensforthe all and singler the said uses ententes and lymitacons of uses and estates therof so signefied and declared by writing as is aforsaid to be voied (except before excepted) shall cease be voied and of none effecte onelie towching all suche and somuche of the said mannors lordships lands tenements and heredita-ments and other the premisses whereof or for or concerning the whiche the said uses ententes and lymitacons of uses or estates before in theis presents declared lymited or expressed shalbe so signefied or declared by writing as is aforsaid to be voied and of none effecte And that then and from thenfforth the said conveiance and assurance so as is aforsaid appointed to be made to the said Lord Cobham Henry Brooke Sir Thos. Cecill Edward Wotton William Fitzwilliams Anthony Cooke ffrannces Bacon Vyncent Skynner and Barnerd Dewhurst and their heires or to the heires of one of them And also all and everie other conveiance and assurannce to be made before the said Laste Daie of November by the said Baron of Burghley to the said Lord Cobham Henry Brooke Sir Thos. Cecill Edward Wotton William Fitzwilliams Anthony Cooke ffrannces Bacon Vyncent Skynner and Barnerde Dewhurst and their heires [shalbe and the said Lord Cobham and the said other persons and their heires] shall from thenfforth forever stand and be seised of and in all suche and somuche of the said mannors lands tenements and hereditaments and other the premises with the appurtenences concerning whiche and whereof suche significacon or declaracon shalbe so made for the ceasing and determyning of the said uses or any of them (except before excepted) to the onelie use of suche person or persons as the said Lord Burghley shall by any writing or writings by him to be subscribed and sealed or by his last will and testament by him to be subscribed lymitt or appointe And if no suche lymitacon or appointment shalbe made Then to the use of the said Lord Burghley his heires and assignes forever Any thinge in theis presents beforemencioned or any conveiances hereafter to be made of the premisses or any parte thereof or any other matter or cause to the contrarie thereof in eny wise notwithstonding And furthermore the said Baron of Burghley for himself his heires and assignes doth grannte and covenante by theis presents to and with the said Lord Cobham Henry Brooke Sir Thomas Cecill Knight Edward Wotton William Fitzwilliams Anthony Cooke ffrannces Bacon Vyncent Skynner and Barnerd Dewhurst their heires executors and adminis-trators That during all the lyfe tyme of the said Lord Burghley he the said Lord Burghley or his assignes shall and will from tyme to tyme out of and with the Rentes yssues and proffittes of the said messuage called Pleasantynes the said Lands meadowes leasowes pastures marshes and hereditaments now or sometymes accompted to be parcell of the mannor of Depehams aforsaid and of the said woodgroundes woodes and underwoodes in Edmonton aforsaid content and pay all and singler the Rentes and quitrentes yssueng out of all and every the premisses before in theis presents mencioned to suche person and persons to whome the same or any of the same shall growe due or thereof and of everie parte thereof shall and will acquite or otherwise upon reasonable requeste save harmeles all and everie other the said lands tenements and hereditaments And that all and singler the lands tenements and hereditaments before in theis presents lymited appointed mencioned or meante to be to or for the Jointure or augmentacion of the Joincture of the said Elizabeth Brooke shalbe by him the said Lord Burghley or his heires from tyme to tyme during all the life of her the said Elizabeth Brooke acquited and discharged or otherwise upon reasonable request saved and kept harmeles or recompensed from and for all and almaner of former conveiances assurannces Estates leases bondes charges Rentes and Incumbrannces whatsoever had or made by the said Lorde Burghley. And he the said Lord Cobham for himself his heires executors and administrators doth by theis presentes for and in consideracion of the mariage aforsaid and in consideracon of the said assurannce and conveiance so to be had and made as is aforsaid covennante and grannte to and with the said Lord Burghley his executores and administratores That he the said Lord Cobham his heires executores or administrators shall and will well and trulie contente and pay to him the said Lord Burghley his executores or administrators the full Some of Two thousand Poundes of good and lawfull Money of England in maner and forme following That is to saie the some of One thousand Poundes parcell thereofe upon the daie of the said mariage so to be had and solemnized as is aforsaid or within foure daies then next following at the Mansion howse of the said Baron of Burghley comonlie called Burghley Howse situate in the Strounde in the Countie of Middlesex And the further some of One other Thousand Poundes residue of the said some of Two Thousand Poundes at the ende of one yere after the said marriage at the said Mansion Howse In Witnes whereof the Parties first abovenamed to theis Indentures Interchanngeably have put their handes and seales the daie and yere first abouewritten.

The Deed, which consists of two parchments each measuring 2 feet by 2 feet 7 inches, is signed "W. BURGHLEY," which signature alone appears at the bottom of the first parchment, on the outer fold of which is written in crabbed writing :—

"Ultimo Maij . . . . Regniæ Elizabeth xxxj^{mo}."

"A Booke for the Joincture of Mrs Elizabeth Brooke who by godes grace is to marie with Robt Cecill Esquier and as for the Inheyritange of the Landes in the said Joincture and dyverse other landes unto the said Robert Cecill and the heires of his body with dyvers remaynders."

"All my landes in Edmonton and Tottenham the Dayrie ferme in Endfelde and Chesthunte Nunrie."

On one of the inner folds appears the following, the signatures being in various handwritings :—

"Sealed and Delivered to the within named Barnard Dewhurste for himselfe and the resideue of the Persons within named in presence of

JO. LOWEN.
H. RAYNARD.
MICHAEL HICKES.
WILLIAM STYLE.
RICH. SHUTE.
RYCHARD BRADSHAGH.
GEO. MASON (?).
HUMFREY PLESSINGTON (Lysons, p. 252).
H^y EDWARDES.
GILBERT WAKERINGE " (Lysons, p. 259).

Facsimile of signature of LORD BURGHLEY.

Facsimile of signature of WILLIAM, SECOND EARL OF SALISBURY. From Deed quoted on p. 6.

Sir Hamon Belknap, Lord Treasurer of Normandy.=Joan (da. and coheir of Sir Thos. Butler of Sudley).

(A)

- William Belknap, had livery of his lands 16 Edw. IV. Ob. 2 Rich. III.

- Henry Belknap of Beccles, co. Suffolk, 3rd son.=Margaret, da. of Richard Knowls. Heir to his brother William. Bur. at Beccles. Will dated 25 June 1488.

- Anne Belknap, coheir to her brother.=Sir Robert Wotton of Boughton Malherbe, co. Kent, born circa 1460. "Knight Porter and Comptroller of Calais." Bur. at Calais. (A 4 and 5)

- Nicholas Wotton. (One of the Privy Council. Ob. 1566. Bur. in Canterbury Cathedral.)

- Sir Edward Belknap, commanded in battle of Stoke, 2 Hen. VII. Constable of Warwick Castle 17 Hen. VII. Will dated 28 March 1520.

- Elizabeth=Sir Philip Cooke of Giddy Hall, co. Essex, Knt. (coheir to her brother). (A)

- Mary=Gerard Danet. (coheir).

- Alice Belknap, coheir, mar. Wm Shelley.

- Sir Edward Wotton.= (Vitâ 29 Henry VIII. Born 1489. Treasurer of the Town and Marshes of Calais.)

- Elizabeth (da. of John Reedstone of Bocton Moncheney).=Thomas Wotton of Boughton Malherbe, co. Kent, born 1521. (1)

- Sir Edward Wotton of Boughton Malherbe. Created 1608 Baron Wotton of Marley, co. Kent (Third-cousin to Robert Cecil's mother.) (2)

- Eleanora, da. of William Finch of Eastwell.=Sir Henry Wotton, Knt.

- Sir William Fitz William of Gaines Park, co. Essex, Knt., and of Milton. Sheriff for London 1506. Ob. 1534.=Anne, da. of John Hawes. (B)

- Sir John Cooke of Giddy Hall, co. Essex, Knt.=Alice (da. and coh. of William Saunders of Banbury).

- Sir John Danet. Issue, Leonard Danet, who inherited a moiety of the Belknap estate.

- Beatrice Cooke.=Richard Ogle of Pinchbeck, Lincoln, son of Richard Ogle by Maria, sister to Sir Wm Fitz William of Milton. (c)

- Audrey Ogle, widow of John Maun of Bolingbroke.=Sir Vincent Skynner. (Mar. 1569 at Bolingbroke.) (Husband to the first-cousin of Rob't Cecil's mother.) (D)

- Sir Francis Bacon, Baron Verulam and Viscount St. Albans (first-cousin to Robert Cecil).

- Sir Wm Fitz William, of Milton and Gaines Park, co. Essex, Knt.=Anne, da. of Sir Richard Sabcotts, of Elton, co. Hunts.

- Anne Fitz William.=Sir Anthony Cooke of Giddy Hall, co. Essex.

- Anne Cooke.=Sir Nich. Bacon, Knt., Lord Keeper.

- Sir Wm Fitz William of Gaines Park, Knt. Ob. 1599.=Anne or Agnes, da. of Sir William Sydney and sister of 1st Earl of Leicester.

- Mildred Cooke, mar. 21 Decem. 38 Hen. VIII.=Sir Wm Cecil, (Lord Burghley). Bur. 29 Aug. 1598 in Westminster Abbey. Ob. 1589. (B)

- Mary, of Peter Cheke. Mar. 8 August 33 Hen. VIII.

- Anne.=Ed. de Vere, 17th Earl of Oxford.

- Robert Cecil (Earl of Salisbury).

- Thomas Cecil (Earl of Exeter), a quo present Marquis of Exeter.

- Susan de Vere, mar. Philip Herbert, Earl of Montgomery.

- A quo Earl of Pembroke.

- Sir William Fitz William, ob. 1618 (second-cousin to Robert Cecil).

- Bridget de Vere, mar. Francis, Lord Norris, of Rycote.

- A quo Lord Abingdon.

- Elizabeth de Vere, mar. 26 June 1594 William, 6th Earl of Derby.

AUTHORITIES.

(A) 1. Dugdale's 'Warwickshire,' p. 409, 1st edition; 2. Morant's 'Essex,' vol. ii, p. 470; 3. 'Essex Visit.,' Harl. Soc., vol. ii, p. 564; 4. Hasted's 'Kent,' vol. i, p. 185; 5. Burke's 'Extinct Peerage.'

(B) 1. Collins' 'Peerage'; 2. Burke's 'Peerage'; 3. 'Essex Visitations,' Harl. Soc.; 4. 'Blackheath,' p. xiii.

(c) 1. 'Genealogist,' vol. iv, p. 261; 2. 'Collectanea Topographica,' vol. vi, p. 194; 3. 'Miscellanea Genealogica et Heraldica,' New Series, vol. i, p. 81.

(D) 1. Metcalfe's 'Visit. of Suffolk.'

Appendix.

It is just 300 years since this Settlement was drawn up with a view to the marriage of Robert Cecil, second son of William, Lord Burghley, with Elizabeth, daughter of William, Lord Cobham, which marriage we know was duly solemnized.

I discovered it among some very old family deeds, and have thought it of sufficient interest—to those at least who are interested in matters historical, genealogical, or antiquarian—to make public. It has been a great interest to me to transcribe it, and also to discover what blood relations there might be between the several parties to the Deed—which relations I have embodied in a short pedigree, by which it will be seen that all the parties to the Deed were related to the expectant bridegroom, with the exception of his future wife's father and brother, and Bernard Dewhurst, Lord Burghley's servant.

The Settlement has its chief interest in the fact that it brings before us the names of some of those who make the history of the reigns of Elizabeth and James the First, consequently it makes it the harder to say anything that is not well known to most readers; and it is with great diffidence that I have ventured to dwell at all upon the lives and characters of such men as Lord Burghley, Robert Cecil, and Francis Bacon; and yet it seemed quite impossible to pass over their names in absolute silence when dealing with the other parties to the Deed. I trust, therefore, that those who read it will kindly bear in mind that I do not for a moment suppose that they will find any new matter in the short sketches which accompany the Deed, and for which I give the following authorities from which the matter has been drawn, except where I specially have mentioned them :—

I. General Dictionary, by Mr. Bayle, translated by Bernard, Birch, and Lockman, published 1734.

II. English History, by Hume and Lord Clarendon.

D

iii. Hasted's History of Kent (Hundred of Blackheath), by Drake (abbreviated "Blackheath" when given as authority).

iv. Metcalfe's Book of Knights and Nicolas's Synopsis of the Peerage.

I take the names of the parties to the Deed as nearly as possible in the order in which they appear in the Pedigree.

SIR WILLIAM FITZWILLIAM, second-cousin to Robert Cecil, was the son of Sir William Fitzwilliam, who served in Ireland either as Lord Justice or as Lord Deputy from 1560—1590, and, who having been as a lad under the tuition and in the service of his mother's kinsman John Russel, first Earl of Bedford and Lord Privy Seal, was thus early brought into connection with a political life, which he began in the reign of Edward VI. under good auspices. His character and attainments enabled him to take advantage of the "hand up" which his kinsman gave him, and he has been honoured by a place among Fuller's 'Worthies of England,' who justly observes that the fact of his having been "five" times Deputy of Ireland is sufficient evidence of his honesty and ability under such a sovereign as Elizabeth. As sole heir to his father, he was possessed of very large estates in the counties of Northampton, Essex, and Lincoln, but as he was so much in Ireland, he probably lived very little at either Gaines Park or Milton, and Collins remarks in his 'Peerage' that he was also Constable of Fotheringay Castle during the time of Mary, Queen of Scots' imprisonment, and that she presented him with a picture of her son James as a mark of her esteem. This of course must have been between two of his appointments as Lord Deputy of Ireland. He chose as his burialplace the family vault in the chancel of Marham or Marholm Church, co. Northants, where his father was buried, and there he was buried in June 1599, where a noble monument, exhibiting the figures of himself and his wife, testifies to his services in Ireland, "as Lord Lieutenant three times, and as Lord Justice five times." His grandfather's sister had married as her second husband Richard Ogle of Pinchbeck, father of Beatrice Cooke's husband. His wife was daughter to Sir William Sydney, and aunt to the first Earl of Leicester; consequently their son Sir William—one of the parties to this Deed—would not only be first-cousin to Robert, Earl of Leicester, but also to the Earl's eldest brother Sir Philip Sydney, whose extreme benevolence and kindness of heart, together with his extraordinary scholarly and military attainments, has made his name so illustrious in English history; but, notwithstanding the help that his relations on both his father's and mother's side could have given him in a public life, Sir William apparently took little part in politics, and probably lived a retired life at one of his places in Essex or Northamptonshire. His sister Margaret married John Byron, ancestor to the Poet, and he himself married Winifred, daughter to Sir Walter Mildmay of Apethorp, co. Northants, Chancellor of the Exchequer; and dying 5 August 1618, was buried with his ancestors at Marham. The pedigree of this family, besides being related at length in Collins's ' Peerage,' appears in the Visitations of Yorkshire, Essex, and Northamptonshire, and is I believe authenticated as far back as the Conquest. From him is descended the present Lord Fitzwilliam.

WILLIAM BROOKE, Lord Cobham of Cobham Hall, co. Kent, father-in-law of Robert Cecil, was summoned to Parliament from 1558 to 1596. His family had inherited this ancient barony and estates through Joan, daughter and sole heir of Sir Reginald Braybroke by his wife Joane de la Pole, granddaughter and heir of John Cobham, the last of that family who bore the title. He was Lord Warden of the Cinque Ports at the death of Queen Mary, and was deputed to announce the accession of Queen Elizabeth to the Spaniards in the Netherlands. Having taken part in the Duke of Norfolk's designs for marrying Mary, Queen of Scots, he was committed to the Tower. Afterwards he was appointed Constable of Dover Castle, Lord Chamberlain, and a Knight of the Garter. By his second marriage with Frances, daughter of Sir John Newton, he had, beside other issue, Henry Brooke (who succeeded him in 1596 as Lord Cobham and as Warden of the Cinque Ports) and George. Both were found guilty and condemned to death as participators in the " Main Plot " and in the " Bye " or " Surprise Plot." The first, led by Sir Walter Raleigh and Henry, Lord Cobham, was a plot to place Arabella Stuart on the throne; the second, in which George alone was concerned, was a design to surprise and imprison James, and to remodel the government. Robert Cecil, hearing of these plots, had the conspirators, including his brothers-in-law, arrested. It was mainly on Henry, Lord Cobham's evidence that Raleigh was implicated, and there were many who held him innocent. George Brooke was executed; his eldest brother lived to undergo the worse fate of a life-long imprisonment in poverty and misery, and ultimately in 1619 a prisoner's death in the Tower. It is asserted that his wife, a daughter of Charles Howard, Earl of Nottingham, although a very wealthy woman, refused to relieve his wants when in prison. He had no issue.

SIR WILLIAM CECIL, LORD BURGHLEY.—As regards this well-known historical character it is unneccessary to say much, and it would be very hard to find anything that is not well known to most readers. He was son of Richard Cecil, Master of the Robes to Henry VIII. and Edward VI., was born 13 September 1520 at Bourne in co. Lincoln, and was educated at the Grammar Schools of Grantham and Stamford, which latter place his grandfather David Cecil, who possessed an estate there, had represented in Parliament in 1525. The name seems to have been variously spelt Sitsilt, Sycill, Cyssel, Cecyll, according to Collins, who finds an ancestor to this family as far back as the reign of William Rufus. The Visitation of Northamptonshire (Harleian Society) taken in 1618 begins the pedigree with one Thomas Cecill of Halterennes, great-grandfather to David Cecil above mentioned : David, by his marriage with Joan, daughter of John Dicons of Stamford, acquired certain estates in co. Lincoln, which were settled on his second son Richard, whose eldest son Sir William inherited them on his father's death in 1553. David Cecil and his son Richard were both buried at Stamford. William proceeded in due course to St. John's College, Cambridge, where he hired the bellringer to call him at 4 A.M. every morning. He gave proof of his ability there in a lecture written in Greek before he was nineteen. A story is also told of him that at this time, when on a visit to his father at Court, meeting two Priests, Chaplains to the Irish Chief O'Neil, he disputed with them in the Latin tongue on the subject of the Pope's supremacy in a most able manner, and that this brought him to the King's notice. He was noted in after life for his staunch Protestant opinions, yet he cleverly escaped the persecution of Mary's reign, even refusing at her hands the bribe, if he would change his religion, of the posts of Secretary of State and Privy Councillor. On the accession of Elizabeth he was offered and accepted both those posts, and in 1572 was appointed Lord High Treasurer, having been created the year before Lord Burghley. He was mainly instrumental in establishing the Protestant religion throughout the country. He is described as a man of middle height, a pleasant face, and a good complexion. He died 4 August 1598, and was in his sixty-ninth year when he signed this Deed.

THOMAS CECIL, only child of Lord Burghley by his marriage with Mary, daughter of Peter Cheke, who died soon after his birth, was born 5 May 1542, and was elected 5 Elizabeth to Parliament for the borough of Stamford, represented nearly forty years before by his great-grandfather. His mother's brother Sir John Cheke, who had been appointed tutor to Edward VI., is said to have been the first to instruct his pupil in the keeping of a journal. He joined Lady Jane Grey's party from religious motives, and acted as her secretary, and in consequence was sent to the Tower ('Blackheath,' p. xxii). He died 1557. Sir Thomas Cecil was knighted at Kenilworth in 1575, and in 1588 volunteered, together with his brother Robert, on board the fleet at the time of the Spanish Invasion. He was made a member of the Privy Council by James I., and in 1605 was created Earl of Exeter, an honour he refused two years before, saying in a letter addressed to Sir John Hubbert, dated 12 January 1603: "I am resolvyd to contente myselfe with this estate I have of a Baron." Beyond performing a few insignificant duties, however, I do not find that he was remarkable for performing anything, except in begetting fourteen children, one of which, Edward, much distinguished as a general, and created Viscount Wimbledon in 1626, is mentioned by Walpole among his 'Noble Authors' as the writer of two MS. tracts on the Art of War. Lord Exeter died 1622, and was buried in St. Paul's Chapel in the Collegiate Church at Westminster (Maitland's 'London,' p. 699): "Thomas Cecill, Comes Exeter, Baro de Burleigh, Ordinis Garterii Eques, Regi Jacobo a Sanctioribus Consiliis, cum clarissimis duabus uxoribus ejus, Dorothea Nevill, ex nobili Domini Latameri Familia, & una ex Cohæredibus prima Uxore: Et Francisca Bridges ex nobili Familia Chandois, secunda Uxore; cum firma spe Resurrectionis hoc in Monumento compositi obdormierunt." The present Marquis of Exeter is descended from his first wife.

ROBERT CECIL, brother to the above, though second son of Lord Burghley, was the only son by his marriage with Mildred, daughter of Sir Anthony Cooke, sometime tutor to Edward VI., whose grandfather, the first to settle at Giddy Hall, co. Essex, was Lord Mayor of London 1463, and whose second son Sir William Cooke settled at Highnam in Gloucestershire (now owned by the Gambier Parrys), which estate his descendants possessed for some generations. Mildred, Lady Burghley, was a most accomplished and well-read woman and a good Latin and Greek scholar; consequently with such a father and such a mother it would have been a remarkable fact had Robert Cecil not been a distinguished man. He was born in 1563, and was therefore in his twenty-sixth year at the time of his marriage. He is stated to have been of a weak constitution and deformed in person ('Biog. Brit.') ; hence probably the nickname of "Little Beagle," given to him by James I. His intellect and knowledge were, however, by no means weak, which is evinced by the part he took in the government during the reigns of Elizabeth and James, in which he shewed himself not only a man of parts, but also fully alive to the desirability of standing well in the estimation of both those actually in power and those likely to become powerful. Well knowing the dislike of the Queen to hearing her probable successor discussed, he had to keep his correspondence with James of Scotland well hidden from her. He, however, was once very nearly discovered. When driving with her at Blackheath they met the post from Scotland. She stopped the coach to receive the packet, but Sir Robert, fearful of a discovery, called quickly for a knife, and cutting the packet open, complained to the Queen that it "smelt ill-favoured by coming out of nasty budgets," and advised that it should be well aired before she saw it; thus taking advantage of his mistress's well-known dislike to evil smells, to turn her attention from his secret dispatches. The chief blot in his character is the part he took in the prosecution of the Earl of Essex and Sir Walter Raleigh, which is too well known to remark on here. It is curious also to note that his hatred for Sir Francis Bacon, his first-cousin, and one of the parties to his marriage settlement, was kept up during the whole of his life. It probably proceeded from jealousy. He was created Baron Cecil 1603, Viscount Cranbourne 1604, Earl of Salisbury 1605. He held the office of Lord High Treasurer during the last four years of his life, when he formed a scheme for providing James with money, and on pretence of raising money for the defence of Ulster he invented the order of Baronetcies, the patent for which was sold for £1095. Hence baronets bear on their arms the bloody hand of Ulster. He died 14th May 1612, and was buried at Hatfield. Notwithstanding all his honours and success in life, he hardly appears to have been a happy man, if one may judge by his words in his last illness to Sir Walter Cope :—" Ease and pleasure quake to hear of death, but my life full of cares and miseries desireth to be dissolved" (Burke's 'Peerage'). A letter to Sir James Harrington the Poet, in 1603, when he was almost in the zenith of his power, is written in much the same tone. Perhaps, like Solomon, he was *blasé* with the world, its riches and honours. By his marriage with Elizabeth Brook he had issue one son William, for whom in April 1591 Queen Elizabeth stood sponsor ('Mis. Gen. et Her.,' New Series, vol. ii., p. 296), and a daughter Frances, married to Henry Clifford, Earl of Cumberland. A third child was born, which cost him the life of his wife, and which probably died at the same time, as I find no further notice of it. The following monumental inscription is quoted by Maitland (p. 699) in his 'History of London' from the Collegiate Church at Westminster :—

> "A Brooke by name the Baron Cobham's child,
> A Newton was she by her mother's side,
> Cecill her husbande this for her did build,
> To prove his love did after death abide ;
> Which tells unto the worldes that after come
> The worldes concepte, whilest here she held a roome ;
> How nature made her wise and well beseeminge
> Witt and condition, silente, trew, and chaste,
> Her vertues rare, wann her much esteeminge,
> In Courte her Soveraigne still with favour graste
> Earth coulde not yealde more pleasing earthye Blisse
> Blest with two babes, the thirde brought her to this."

Robert Cecil's signature as Viscount Cranbourne and also as Lord Salisbury is given by Drake in his edition of 'Hasted's Kent: Blackheath Hundred' (1886), being Nos. 68 and 69; also his father's (134), and his brother-in-law's (66), as Lord Cobham.

The history of FRANCIS BACON is too well known to require many words. He was the youngest son of Sir Nicholas, the first Lord Keeper invested with the power of Lord Chancellor, by his marriage with Anne Cooke, who, with her sister Lady Burghley, was alike "eminent for her skill in the Latin and Greek tongues." He was born at York House in the Strand 22 January 1560 (Old Style). As quite a child he seems to have shewn, by his apt and clever answers, that he had no mean ability, and Dr. Rawley tells us of the delight with which Queen Elizabeth used to set herself to talk with him, calling him "The young Lord Keeper." His father died in 1579 intestate ; consequently, although he had collected a large sum of money to buy land wherewith to endow his youngest son, Francis had to content himself with his proportion alone, which left him with very narrow means. On the death of his brother Anthony, many years afterwards, the Manor of Gerhambury near St. Albans came to him. Anthony was the only other son born to Sir Nicholas by his wife Anne Cooke, although by his first marriage with Jane, daughter of William Ferneley, he had three sons, the eldest of which was created a baronet

1662, which baronetcy became extinct on the death of his grandson twenty-three years later, and three daughters ('Visitation of Suffolk,' by Metcalfe). Francis began his education in public affairs by going with Sir Amyas Paulet to France, during which absence his father died. He entered himself at Gray's Inn, and in 1593 first entered Parliament, was knighted 1603, and appointed successively Solicitor-General and Attorney-General, and one of the Privy Council, Lord Keeper 1617, Lord Chancellor and Baron Verulam 1610, Viscount St. Albans 1621, and is most erroneously styled by the thoughtless and ignorant "Lord Bacon," among the former of whom Hume is conspicuous.

During the first part of his life, his uncle Lord Burghley and his cousin Robert Cecil were, curiously enough, his chief enemies, and the unfortunate Earl of Essex his greatest benefactor, actually giving him a small estate, namely, "Twickenham Park, and its garden of Paradise, worth more, Bacon tells us, than £1800, a large sum in those days," though that same estate has been valued at £100,000 in the present time; and yet Francis Bacon, owing to his moral cowardice, appeared against his old friend as Queen's Counsel at his trial, and was consequently instrumental in his death. The appeal to the people by the Government in defence of their sentence was entrusted to Bacon, it is said, by the contrivance of Robert Cecil, and brought upon him the contempt of the whole nation. It is curious that Lord Burghley should have chosen him as a party to his son's marriage settlement, considering the assumed contempt in which he openly professed to regard him. His chief fault, which appears throughout his life, was the moral cowardice spoken of above, and this was eventually the main instrument in his ruin, for he was evidently, from all one can gather from an impartial review of his life, a mere tool in the hands of James and his favourite Buckingham, in the matter of the patents and monopolies. His character in this affair is open to criticism, and much has been written about it. But even with the strong desire which all who love his writings must have not to see his name roughly handled, an unbiassed person must acknowledge that with the headpiece he had, Bacon was certainly most culpable in becoming a mere tool in the hands of the unscrupulous, a part generally played by the fool, hardly by the wise man. He was very reckless, too, in the expenditure of his money, spending much upon the outward show of many servants and magnificent grandeur during the last few years of his life. He died in comparative poverty on Easter

Day, 9 April 1626, from the effects on a by no means strong constitution of sleeping in a damp bed at Lord Arundel's. These words appear in his will: " My name and memory I leave to foreign nations, and to mine own countrymen after some time be passed over." And it is certainly for his writings that now, after nearly 300 years, the name of Francis Bacon is loved and reverenced by his countrymen; for they appeal to almost every feeling of human nature, and in writing of him we may well convert the words of Shakespeare, and say, with respect to his writings—

> " The good that men do lives after them,
> The evil is oft interred with their bones."

SIR EDWARD WOTTON was third-cousin to Lady Burghley and Lady Bacon, and chiefly shines with a reflected light as being half-brother to Sir Henry Wotton, whose name has been made familiar to us by Izaak Walton, whose charming life of him gives many details of his family. It is unnecessary to quote much from so well-known a book, especially as Sir Henry is not the subject of this paper (cf. also Chambers's ' Book of Days,' 30 March). Bocton Hall, the old home of the Wottons, is described by Walton as being, together with the church, within a fair park. The family history given by the same writer begins with Sir Robert, the first in my pedigree, and in giving the account of Sir Edward, he says " Sir Edward was knighted by Queen Elizabeth, and made a comptroller of her Majesty's household. ' He was,' saith Camden, ' a man remarkable for many and great employments in the state during her reign, and sent several times ambassador into foreign nations.' After her death, he was by King James made comptroller of his household, and called to be of his Privy Council, and by him advanced (1603) to be Lord Wotton, Baron of Merley in Kent, and made Lord Lieutenant of that county." He owed his advancement to his distant cousin Robert Cecil. He married Hester, daughter and coheir of Sir William Puckering of Oswald Kirk, co. York, and was succeeded by his son Thomas, who dying in 1630 without issue male, the title became extinct. One or two of his family were dreamers of dreams which are said have come true, which calls forth the remark from Izaak Walton that they seemed to be a family beloved of God.

SIR VYNCENT SKYNNER, son and heir of John and grandson of Robert Skynner (who died 1536), was over three years old at the time of his father's

B

death, on 11th of October 1545. His mother was Elizabeth, daughter of John Fairfax of Swarby, co. Lincoln ('Mis. Gen. et Her.,' New Series, vol. i., pp. 81 and 177; also 'Herald and Genealogist,' vol. vi., p. 621). His father inherited lands in Thorpe and Wainfleet, co. Lincoln. Sir Vincent is, however, described as of Thornton College, co. Lincoln; was M.P. for Truro, co. Cornwall, and Boston, co. Lincoln; and was knighted at Theobalds 7 May 1603. His first wife was, as stated in the pedigree, Audry, daughter of Richard Ogle, and widow of John Man of Bolingbroke, at which place they were married 16 Jan. 1569–70 (cf. 'Collectanea Topographica,' etc., vi., 194; and 'Genealogist,' iv., 261). By this marriage he appears to have had no children; but by his marriage with Elizabeth, daughter of William or Robert Fowkes, and widow of Henry Middlemore, both of Enfield (Harleian Society, xxv., pp. 264 and 300), he had a son William, also of Thornton College and Lincoln's Inn, who by his marriage with Bridget, second daughter of Sir Edward Coke, Lord Chief Justice, had, with others, a son Edward, also of Thornton College. He and his brother Henry are mentioned as kinsmen in the will of Sir Henry Fairfax, the last Prior of Kyme, co. Lincoln, dated 25 June 1560 (Maddison's 'Lincoln Wills,' p. 76).

BARNERD DEWHURST, described in this Settlement as Servant, and in a wonderful Latin inscription in Cheshunt Church as Secretary, to Lord Burghley, appears to have settled himself at Cheshunt, which he would have known well when in the service of Lord Burghley at Theobalds. The monument claims for him a Lancashire ancestry, probably Dewhurst of Alston (Dugdale's Visitation, 1664, published by the Chetham Society), and runs thus:

Deposita Barnardi Dewhurst arm:
Ex Familia Dewhurstorum e Lancastrensi
Argo (*sic*) oriundi olim Gulielmo Cecilio
Baroni de Burghley Summo Thesaurario
Anglia Secretarii qui obiit 20 Dec: 1596
Anno suo climacterico 63. Thomæ Dewhurst
Filii primogeniti qui obiit 7 Jan: 1612 Anno
ætat: 35. Barnardi Dewhurst Equitis Auratis,
filii ejus quarti qui obiit 24 Sept. 1617 Anno ætat. 35.
Johannis Dewhurst filii ejus quinti qui obiit 2 Ju. 1616
Anno ætat. 24. Prudentiæ Dewhurst uxori Roberti
Dewhurst armig. filii predicti Barnardi secundi
filiæ Thomæ Equitis Auratis quæ obiit 24 Ju. 1621

Anno ætat. 29. Annæ Dewhurst uxor secundi prædict.
Roberti filiæ Rogeri Dye Mercatoris Londiniensis
quæ obiit 10 Ju. 1631 Anno ætat. 28.   Predictus
autem Robertus Dewhurst Custos Brevium de Banco
Regis est adhuc superstis suo tamen ordine
depositurus qui postea obiit quarto Maii
1645 ætat. 68.

Chauncy's ' Herts,' vol. i., p. 591.

In his pedigree (Visitation of Herts, 1634) his son is described as of
Cheshunt Nunnery, and Chauncy asserts that he bought it of Lord Denny,
which is doubtful.   I have discussed this on page 9.   The following pedigree
will set forth what further information I can obtain of this family.   See
' Topographer and Genealogist,' vol. i., 233 ; and Harleian Society, vol. **xxv.**

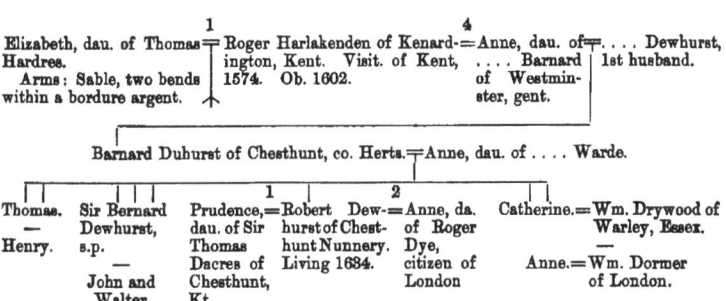

Lightning Source UK Ltd.
Milton Keynes UK
UKHW020607171219
355533UK00005B/836/P

9 781377 232751